SENTENCED TO LOVE

The Challenges of Loving During Lockup

Joshua Harris

TO THE STRUGGLE

CONTENTS

PROLOGUE

My First Love

My mother was my first love. She was strict, yet soft and sweet. Though she had a heart of gold, she was always on the hunt for bullshit. If you were stuck in a jam and needed money, she'd give you her last even if she didn't have it to give. But soon as you were out of her sight, her wheels would start churning, often spewing one of her colorful expressions. "She better not be doing no foolishness with my money", or "I know how to get my money back if it comes to that".

My mother was the strongest woman I've ever known. She would work a double shift, shop for the house, go to the Post Office, and be back home to raise 5 kids, only to get 4 hours of sleep before doing it again the following day. She didn't drink, get high, or even had much of a social life outside of the occasional spades game with long-time friends from church. With all we've put her through, I commend her for not taking a little something "to take the edge off". The resiliency she showed after losing my father and soldering on, that's comparable to none. She never remarried or even dated. Though many men made their advances, she never entertained such gestures. When I would ask her about dating she would always say, "I don't need a man when I got God. Jesus is my man". And she truly believed it.

I can't imagine such a loss as experienced by my mother. I've lost many people I cared deeply for, but to lose the person you planned to spend the rest of your life with; to embark on this thing called life with someone and have that stolen from you that have to hit differently.

It wasn't all cotton candy and teddy bears, my parents had their disputes-both verbal and physical. I remember waking up one morning, I was no older than 9, and both of them were tussling in the living room. With wide and deranged eyes my father demanded I leave the room. Without a second thought, I ran to the open kitchen window and yelled, "Police! Police! My daddy fighting my mommy". He then quickly lifted my tiny body from the window into the hallway before fleeing the apartment. As I made my way to my mother, she hugged me, assuring me that all was well.

I also remember waking up to a "Daffy Duck" looking daddy one morning. As the story goes, after one of my parent's "disputes", my father drunkenly fell into one of his comatose sleeps. This bout was over for him but not my mother. While sleeping, my mother leaned in towards my father until they were nose to nose and bit down viciously onto his lips. Seeing him on the following day one would've easily assumed he'd had an allergic reaction of some sort because of his swollen sausage size lips, but we knew who had the allergies: My mother was allergic to his bullshit and wasn't putting up with any of it. That was my mother; that was my first love.

A.T.D which was abbreviated for an alternative to detention was just that. This was some weird probation school that was the last stop before Juvenile detention. All of the students here were mandated by the courts. The school was run by certified probation officers, and we were under the same supervision as everyone else in the State of New York on probation. We were all given curfews, subjected to random drug testing, and were required to have absolutely no police contact.

I knew she was in trouble when we locked eyes. Smooth

brown complexion, high cheekbones, and the most intense eyes I've ever seen. She wore a red Nautica bubble jacket and Timberland boots. With a resemblance to Nia Long and the swagger of Def Loaf, I knew I was in love. Not puppy love, but right then and there I knew one day she would become my wife. Without yet uttering a word to one another, we both knew it. It was inevitable. Her name was Rita and we met in A.T.D. Out of all the unlikely places, our misguided paths crossed due to our legal woes.

For 3 days we watched each other. Speaking with only our eyes, we told one another everything we needed to know: She was lost and didn't want to be alone is what hers revealed; as mines told her, I knew who I was but with her I knew who I could become. And at the end of the third day, right before we received our metro cards, the ice was broken. "What you in here for?" I asked.

"Me and my friends beat some girls up", she replied. *Yes you did,* I thought to myself. This 5-foot-nothing munchkin, I knew she was a firecracker. This was my Bonnie.

"Where you from?" I asked.

"I'm from Harlem, why?"

Hearing her slight attitude made me want her even more. Plus, she was from Harlem. I had to have her.

"Nah, I'm from Harlem too. I just wanted to know what train you're catching to make sure I get a seat next to you". Fun Fact: All of the Iceberg Slim I read in Chicago had equipped me with more game than EA Sports. I had all of the lines: "Did you know my favorite letter in the alphabet is U?" It's corny but highly effective.

Rita and I caught an uptown 3 train while continuing to make small talk. We were completely unpassed by the horde of people crammed around us; it was as though they didn't exist, as if we were the only two boarding. Knowing the train would eventually reach our departing destinations, I wanted us to depart together. For some reason, I asked if she smoked, and not to my surprise she did. "They got some good chocolate (type of weed) in my hood if you want to smoke something". I said. Though I no longer smoked, I wasn't ready to say goodbye. And neither was she.

"Just smoke right?" She shot back. I assured her my intention was only to smoke. 145th St. here we come.

No girl ever had me like this. I didn't know how to roll a blunt nor even wanted to smoke, yet I was willing to risk my freedom for a girl I'd just met. What drew me to her, even more, was that she was willing to risk the same. One dirty urine in A.T.D. could result in a court remand at our next appearances.

As we exited the 145th St. train station, I heard a familiar voice yell out to me from behind "Lil Johnny Cat". Since my brother Jonathan and I resembled each other people often called me Lil Johnny Cat, his moniker. It was Fudge, the neighborhood weed man. This must've been a sign from the Heavens. I quickly made the purchase, brought 2 vanilla dutches, and proceeded to my building.

Entering in my building I could tell Rita was nervous. I could only imagine her reaction once she learned that we would have to smoke on the roof. Mama Harris wasn't with the company. I was just hoping the designated smoking area wouldn't deter her. One of the things working in my favor, surprisingly, the loitering crackheads had found another hangout. Being that the entrance door to my building was always broken, my building was often the crackhead headquarters. Their absence would at least make things a bit bearable.

"What apartment do you live in?" she asked after walking past the 4th floor.

"I live on the 2nd floor but we gotta smoke upstairs", omitting the actual location.

 The roof just sounded too creepy.

Inside the foyer of the roof, I pulled out a $20 bill and proceeded to break up the weed. We stood silent, again, speaking with only our eyes. Watching her roll that blunt was setting off my teenage hormones. At that age, the plopping of our cats jumping in my lap did the same thing. Don't judge me.

As the weed entered my lungs everything I hated about smoking started to hit me-the giggles, the paranoia, it was all taking a toll on me. I guess she sensed it suggesting we wedge open the roof's door for some air. It was just what I needed.

"Do you have a boyfriend?" I asked.

Surprisingly, she told me the truth that she did. She was too much of a catch not to. Too bad for him; the only thing that mattered at that moment was us. *Should I do it?* I thought to myself. *Man fuck it*, I went in for the kiss. Just like in the white movies "when two people lose all inhabitation, we gave into our indulgences. With great passion and intensity, we were making out like the white people in those "white movies". Not even a loitering crackhead could've ruined the moment. I didn't even taste the aftermath of her mouth from the combination of weed and cigarettes, often resulting in "cottonmouth" – the dry, stale state of heavy smoking.

Our heated make-out session led us to tug fiercely at each other's zippers. Once my fingers found her love below she released a subtle moan. Everything seemed so perfect. Though this wasn't the ideal setting, we were about to make love. I felt it. With her jeans halfway down her knees, I slowly entered her from behind. She felt better than I could've imagined. She felt like warm honey. With each stroke, she'd squeeze my hand.

This was our moment, and nothing was going to ruin it. Before the creation of either one of us, this moment was written for us. For God created us for one another. And approximately 15 strokes in she jumped off me, fixing herself.

This could not be happening; everything was so perfect. The stars were aligned and the moon was singing. I wondered frantically what could've ruined our moment. Was it a rat? They too, were common in my building. Was it because I wasn't wearing a condom? *"Please don't let it be because of a loitering crackhead"*, I thought to myself.

"I'm sorry, I can't do this", she said. "I have to go". Lost and confused, I told her I understood and that it was all right. I gave her cab fare and walked her to the corner to flag down a taxi. For the life of me I couldn't figure out what went wrong. Feeling defeated, I took my little blue balls into the house. "Hey, son," my mother said as I entered the apartment. "How was school today?"

"I need a hug Ma", certainly my mother had smelled the marijuana on me but didn't make a fuss about it. I was such a troubled kid she was just happy I made it home. Inside my mother's embrace, I suddenly felt what she would often describe when asked about dating and remarrying. I already had that.

The profoundness of the relationship between Mother and I was everlasting. It was all that I would ever need. What was unforeseeable, was the womanizing traits I would develop and the plethora of hearts I would leave for others to mend by hoisting my mother to a standard and status that placed unrealistic expectations on my future love interests. My mother was undoubtedly my first love and why I have "mommy issues".

In my earlier years, I was so used to compartmentalizing personal issues and traumatic aspects of my life that none of it ever got addressed. Love and pain are one in the same - one can't truly experience one without experiencing the other. My mother spoiled me rotten out of love. I would get suspended from school and get Jordans. Unbeknownst to me at the time, it led me to not take accountability for my actions; it made me so full of myself that the opinion of others-especially women-were second to mine. I can't speak of the simple aesthetics of love without speaking of its connection to pain. And though my mother is my first love, her love is the crux of my pain. The duality of both – my pain and her love - is also why an 18-year prison sentence didn't break me. It is also what led me to the most profound love of all: The love of MY LIFE (Self-love) that is the same due to the love of my wife.

CHAPTER # 1

HOW I MET YOUR MOTHER

My wife and I met at an employee holiday party at the Gramercy Park Hotel. It was the day of her birthday, making our encounter even more memorable. Before our meeting, I would often see her entering in hotel's cafeteria, as I sat in the rear with the other dispensable hotel stewards. She never noticed me, nor did I even want her to. Seemingly always dressed in pantsuits, Candice exuded a sense of professionalism and legitimacy that was completely foreign to me. Though this was my first real job, I was far from the working type. It may have looked as if I was making an honest living; to the unassuming eye, I was making a dishonest dollar at the same time. I was selling ecstasy to several hotel staffers.

Legitimacy and Professionalism: Two characteristics that Candice undoubtedly embodied and two traits I was the complete opposite of. She seemed so unobtainable for someone like me; so when I decided to shoot my shot at the holiday party, something in me said *Don't fuck this up*. It was bad enough that I looked out of place: Everybody was in formal attire while on the other hand, I wore a hoodie and sneakers. Though confident of my physical attributes, my insecurities lied within what couldn't be seen. For I simply viewed myself as a miscreant only worthy of what's been misrepresented as the "Trap Queens" of the world. I just felt she was out of my league.

"Hello is this seat taken?" I asked as Candice sat solemnly

alone on a couch. She was wearing this sweater dress thingy. I didn't like it one bit; I hated it. But I liked her. I liked her nose and lips and her naturally long hair, but most of all I liked the bio I'd created in my head from the first time I saw her: she was a rose in full bloom, not yet aware of her beauty; she had been taken advantage of one too many times still searching to find her voice; she was the saint that would save this sinner. Ultimately, I felt she was created for me.

"You can have a seat. No one is sitting here" she replied. Her voice was so soothing and hypnotizing. Her words were just how I'd imagine-like melodic notes with each syllable. After about 30 minutes of intense dialogue, we shared information and made plans. That was how I met the love of my life.

When I met Candice I was probably the worst version of myself. I had just dodged a 30-year sentence for attempted murder and robbery in Florida, where I'd also picked up an ecstasy habit. Not to mention I was recently unhappily married. My life had no sense of direction. Too many, the acquisition of someone as cultured and driven as Candice would've been considered God-send and maybe she was. I was just lost-getting high to balance my lows.

I loved spending time with Candice, which made it easy to fall in love with her. Every week we had plans. We went to movies, restaurants, comedy clubs, museums and Atlantic City frequently. I truly valued our time. And I think she did as well.

On our first date, I took her to Barnes and Nobles (I'm a fan of literature, what can I say), the movies followed by some drinks at the Westside Diner. Time went by so fast that neither of us wanted the night to end. Sharing an apartment with my then-wife, I made up a story about having unruly roommates and didn't want to expose her to that. One of us suggested a hotel; she suggested paying. She was independent and didn't need a man to take care of her. This was intimidating yet I was intrigued. I wanted to eat her butt. Don't judge me. I wasn't this manic-ass eater with an insatiable appetite. She just did everything to me even when she did nothing. Plus, she was easy on the eyes; we looked good together.

Candice was unlike any woman I've ever been with. Though she was college educated and way more mature than I was, she never made me feel less than. At times I didn't feel worthy. My sense of inferiority came from truly understanding the quality of the woman I had. Seeing and knowing who she was painfully reminded me just who I wasn't.

Two months into our relationship I enrolled into A.S.A. Community College. I wanted to earn her. Though I was still battling my demons-drugs and alcohol and my involvement in the streets-something in me so badly wanted better for her. She deserved it. From the very first time I saw her; I wanted to protect and provide for her; I wanted a life full of kids and a home to call our own with her; I wanted to give her a part of me only a few knew - the good. The part that was selfless and loving. The part that was created for her.

Eventually, I came clean about my marriage; well, she kind of caught me. I'd been used to removing my ring before Candice and I would meet and forgot one day.

"What's is that on your finger?" she asked. Ever so skilled, I quickly tucked my hand into my pocket, literally removing the ring single-handedly only to reappear ring-less.

What ring? I answered. Although I could tell she was upset, I refrained from asking her about it. It was movie night, we were happy, and I'm sure a part of her didn't want to know in some way.

Later on, that night, while at the movie, I just knew I had to tell her. I couldn't afford to lose her and cared too much to lie. I thought about how I would feel not to be able to have this with her anymore; I thought about how she enjoyed my odd sense of humor while playing tour guide on our walks through Harlem; "This is where they shot Paid In Full. And this is where they shot my man Jose".

Though telling her wasn't going to be easy, not telling her would've been even harder. "Joshua, take what time you need to take care of your business. I'm not a home wrecker and will be here when you finish". I loved her even more, and soon after ended my prior relationship officially.

It didn't take long before things were quite domesticated between the two of us. In no time we were living together, had our daughter, and expecting a boy. Candice had a son from a previous relationship, and I had both a son and daughter from one as well. But now I felt like my world was complete. I had everything I ever wanted and just knew it was only up from here.

Everything that goes up must come down: The story of my life. Just after 2 years of being together I was arrested and charged with murder. How could I've let this happen? Within 2 years I was slowly becoming the man I've always envisioned myself to be, now I was facing a possible death sentence. How could I do this to Candice and the kids and even myself? But all things happen for a reason; what could've ended with me being sentenced to death turned out to me being sentenced to love.

Through this journey, I've discovered a lot, not only about myself but about my partner as well. I've also met a lot of beautiful minds along the way whose journey will forever be intertwined with my own. As I share pieces of their plight that they've shared with me, I share with you my journey. This is "Sentenced to Love".

CHAPTER # 2

MANIPULATION VS. WOMANIPULATION

Growing up, I've often heard women say "Never trust a man in jail, they're master manipulators". I heard this so often before entering into prison that I began to believe it, never giving the benefit of doubt until I was labeled as a manipulator. When the stigma is on us we're quick to cry foul - at least I was.

One of the discoveries I learned much later in my sentence, manipulation often gets misplaced without validity of a justifiable claim. I'm not saying guys in prison aren't manipulative; I've seen the most crafty cons at their highest form of tricky: I once saw a guy get caught in the visiting room with another woman by his wife and flipped the whole script on her. He told her he had to "butter the other girl up" to get an affidavit from her. Guess what? She bought it. She even went as far as to befriend his side chick who was undoubtedly along with his deceitfulness. In regards to this example, no good ass, two-timing manipulator is completely warranted; however, in some instances, can the act of manipulative behavior be justified due to one's conditioning?

Before I embark on a phrase I coined to be **womanipulation**, an undoubtedly controversial term, I'd like to touch more on manipulation and the justification of perceived deceitfulness. In America, when one is accused of a crime before a trial can ensue, the judge must first deem the defendant fit to stand trial. If the defendant is found unfit, the offense doesn't go away or is forgiven, but more sensitive accommodations are made until the said defendant is fit to stand trial. I know many of you are probably wondering where I'm going with this. How does criminal consequence and mental health tie in with manipulative behavior? From the judicial standpoint, it is immoral to condemn someone for a crime who is not of sound mind. They say it's cruel and unethical. And I agree.

Prison is an abnormal environment. From inadequate medical care to the threat of violence from officers and inmates, especially with the stigma of rape associated with this environment, prison isn't for the faint of heart. It takes a lot to make it out. And though the objective for anyone entering prison should always be getting out, soon for those entering, this objective becomes altered to include surviving each day in order to make it out.

In the confines of a single-man cell, one still isn't truly safe. I believe sometimes in life in order to elevate we must isolate. Whether it be from friends and family to work, the nuances of life at times can be overwhelming. But how do we isolate from ourselves (the incarcerated)? How does someone erase the vicious stabbing witnessed just a few feet away? Or the guy who just hung himself after learning his wife was leaving him. And most of all, how does one erase the inner thoughts that comes from within that single-man cell? Sure, a single-man cell can protect one from the dangers lurking outside, but it does nothing to defend from the most dangerous of threats that lie within: you and your thoughts can be more challenging than any obstacle ever imagined.

I commend the Hip Hop culture and celebrities such as Pete Davidson and Charlemagne the God for bringing awareness to mental health. Unfortunately, it isn't as prioritized to the incarcerated as it is to the rest of the world. We don't have such proud supporters and activism. Mental health is still an ostracized subject here that many wish to stay away from, healthcare professionals included.

When survival is the goal every day; and the undiagnosed and unaddressed PTSD one is likely to develop; when you come to the realization that you might have to become who you're not to achieve that goal; when all of the psychological trauma endured conditions you to separate from worldly beliefs and adopt the abnormal customs needed to survive this world; when this is your life, it becomes difficult to balance the abnormal behaviors learned to survive prison from the normal worldly behaviors taught simply to coexist. And often, the profoundness of it all is more felt amongst our interaction with the liberated. Especially our liberated lovers.

Ladies, when a relationship in prison doesn't work out as planned, and you think about how attentive he was and the packages you sent, and the money spent, it's only natural to feel taken advantage of. Understandably, but it doesn't mean the man was a manipulator. The attentiveness of a man in prison isn't an act or tactic, but is done completely against his will, despite his intentions. If you've been fed liver every day for 5 years then one day had been given steak, subconsciously, you would know everything about that steak - from how it was prepared, tasted and even the day you had it. *It was a Tuesday*. The attentiveness wasn't planned; it's because no matter how well or under-cooked the steak (Please excuse the analogy. In no way do I view you all as a piece of meat), that steak was meaningful and memorable.

Now, it's gonna hurt me to admit this, but I do believe they're some prisoners whose intentions aren't the best, which warrants the label manipulator and every other deplorable name one can think of. I also believe some perceived manipulative behaviors can stem from an abnormal conditioning, that is largely dependent on surviving in a world where might trumps right and morality doesn't exist. I'm not saying the heartache and pain of such failed relationships should be forgiven; I'm just saying the psychological toll taken due to this type of abnormal conditioning should be taken into consideration before both labeling one a manipulator and embarking on such a relationship. It'll save a lot of women from unknowingly being participants in what I call womanipulation - the subconscious act of self-manipulation caused by an oversight of understanding personal behavior and those being shown due to a misplaced sense of validation, expectations, and wishful thinking. The mind only works two ways: either with us or against us.

    I can still hear my wife saying "Somebody else in the group broke up today", referring to the locked-up love such as ours, from one of her many online prison support groups. This seemed like a weekly occurrence. And as expected; I would reassure her that we would be different, as if we were the exception. I truly believed it. Needless to say, my claims did little to ease her concern. It was hard to not have doubt when nothing or no one was giving you a reason to be hopeful. Not even me. See, early on, I couldn't see past the trees in the forest and wasn't as upfront with Candice as I should have been. I was also skeptical if we would make it to the other side or end after I was released, as she'd witnessed almost every month in her groups.

    When entering "prison relationships (I hate this term)" or any relationship for that matter, there are many factors that not only influence our efforts but also our expectations. How people meet plays greatly in how womanipulation can affect women. One should never feel obligated to be in a relationship solely out of love for another person but love for themselves as well as having a keen understanding of what love is. Having a warm body in the bed next to you isn't love. Having all the monetary delights of the world loses its value (superficial) if you don't have anybody to share it with. And the beauty and sustainment of this love isn't received through obligation, but earned and deserved through self-validation: knowing your effort, and your worth is your greatest defense to not only protect your heart but guide it. All who choose to "ride it out" and "hold us down", it's damn near impossible - especially for the incarcerated with good intentions – to not feel a sense of obligation to ensure those "happily ever afters". I know I did.

In here, my love language changed and no longer simply consisted of words of affirmation and physical touch. Since being incarcerated, they were soon replaced by gifts and acts of service-visits, packages, and even extracurricular services– the things consistent with prison expectations. The emphasis on expectations is the disregard of acknowledging what we have. And by expecting to fulfill my "obligation" of ensuring our "happily ever after" and for her to know my newfound love languages, it was going to be impossible that my efforts would be well received without a doubt.

Now having expectations and a sense of obligation, with newly discovered love languages, by not communicating this not only contributed to but also validated both of our doubts. We were now becoming conscious of our worth, what we were being shown, as well as our efforts. Only being conscious and exhaustingly communicating these things we were able to break new ground, and that she was able to avoid the pitfalls of womanipulation.

The most rewarding rewards of all come from the effort. Given my new wife and I met before my incarceration, one would assume my effort and commitment to making it work would probably be more of a priority compared to couples meeting through pen-pal services or "jail hookups". I wouldn't fully agree with that; however, I do believe expectations of such an obvious gives more of an incentive - (However one of my favorite words). The profoundness of one's incentive is based on one intentions, and intention isn't cultivated by time together but solely of individuality: who are you when you all are a part? Who you were before meeting? And ultimately who are you?

From my talks with incarcerated individuals who have either been part of jail hookups, pen-pal services, or both, they all agree you only get one shot at making a good first impression. Some seduce through deep 4-page letters consisting of philosophical dialogue and desires out of life; on visits, others try to leave their mark through visual and other mannerisms of attraction - your best-fitting clothes on an appealing physique with smell goods seems to be the more enacted choice.

You should see how these guys prep for an initial encounter with a "potential". They brush their hair (in some cases, what little that's left) 1000 strokes in each direction; they ask to borrow jewelry and other tidbits; they practice how they'll walk up and talk (mock impression); and lastly, what I've even participated in, do a bunch of push-ups right before to get a 'pump'.

As for the liberated ladies, they have their own similar rituals. They change into their "good clothes" upon reaching the facility; they make sure their hair and outfits are up to par; and most of all, they hide their crazy. Nah, I'm just playing, but there are several behaviors we employ and omit for showcasing not what's expected (it's another E word but not that E word), but what's exceptional. This goes especially for the incarcerated. What better way to make convicted of murder and sentenced to 25 to life make one say "But he different though". I should change the obvious ethnic tone. Or "Rebecca, people can change. Richard, don't know you from college". We display what's needed to get what we want, but our intentions and efforts will ultimately determine exactly what it is we have.

Often, with first impressions, it's very difficult to confirm one's intentions; it's even harder to identify the intentions of others when already affected by womanipulation. As honest as it "may sound harsh and superficial, I don't know how many times I've said to myself "What are they doing with each other" after seeing an unlikely pairing. Now, I'm not saying opposites don't attract, but under certain circumstances, it's safe to enter with caution. I've witnessed pen-pal encounters blossom into marriage, producing children and flourishing greatly. I've also witnessed, many circumstantial relationships ending as the opposers (friends and family) of such relationships predicted, leaving one to be hurt, angry, and feeling utterly manipulated. No offense, but when you see a Michael B Jordan "kissy face" with a Lunell, that original E word comes back into play. This time it isn't shared amongst the relationship participants, but everyone else- and some even say, "I did not expect this". And I think it's largely due to our innate and instinctual ability to both reason and be opinionated.

Whether it's the bag (prison contraband), money, visits, or any other prison-appraised service, one of the ways to help determine one's intent is monitoring the dispense of those luxuries and asking the hard question: What do I want from my locked away lover? And what do they want from me? By doing so, can provide all there is for one to see. This isn't to say you shouldn't express your love for your locked-away lover with such luxuries, but by carefully managing what you give can help you better identify what it is you get.

Now, a lot of guys might want to make a move on me when they see me in the yard. I can hear it now, "Get off that Steve Harvey shit. I ain't get a package in months because of your book". On the flip side to withholding these 'incarcerated comforts' that many of us prisoners unjustly learn to equate with love, the removal of these things can make us feel unvalued and lost of interest.

When one is affected by womanipulation, it doesn't matter how the two of you met. Often, the main influencer of womanipulation is insecurity. Whether it's age, weight, or just the fear of being alone, these insecurities contribute to one's conditioning of womanipulation. It is our job (locked-up lovers) to give our lovers the support needed to "help" them feel secure, but we can't "make" our lovers feel secure. That is something you all have to do on your own.

In regards to the profoundness of conditioning, I would like to tell you about my friend Star: I've witnessed my friend Star, who has endured a great deal of unimaginable trauma – sexual violence, abusive relationships, familial dysfunction, etc. sabotage every relationship she has ever been in, especially with those who showed potential. And at every turn, her suitors would take her back. She would tell them of her unfortunate experiences and finish with her two most overused words: (or crutches as I like to call them): "I'm Broken".

Now, I don't believe she was trying to garner sympathy by purposely being manipulative; it was just easier for them to understand and connect the dots of conditioning because her story is and all too familiar one. If we, as a people can employ patience and understanding without chastisement in her case, how can we not employ the same for the complex behaviors of someone conditioned to an abnormal environment such as prison? Just something to think about.

CHAPTER # 3

THE BACK-UP PLAN

I like to think of myself as being very secure when it comes to my relationship with my wife. And honestly, I am. I just wasn't always secure with myself. Letting my mind run rampant with stories of abandonment as well as reflecting on the mishandling of my relationship with Candice before my arrest, I couldn't think of a reason she should stay.

Though I didn't know what this journey would entail, I knew it wouldn't be easy. I also knew I didn't want to put her through such a tough ordeal because of my poor decisions. So I did what most guys routinely do in similar situations: I made her feel guilty by telling her that she could leave. I had to give her an option (as if it was mine to give). However, I think I only felt compelled to give her an "option" because I distastefully had another option. I had a backup plan.

When I was arrested I was 23 years old. Candice and I already had a daughter together and were expecting a boy. I'd cheated in the past and was found in a couple of questionable situations that would assume that I was possibly living foul. Though I wasn't, I'm not alone when I say like many of us, have one of those that we know we could always selfishly have. They're like reserves, or the people no matter what will always answer that 4 am call: "Hey Big Head", or "You up?" Sounds familiar? And though I wasn't passing through the doors of infidelity with said reserves, I did leave the door ajar.

When you find the right one that should be it right? There shouldn't be any backup plans. In a perfect world, yes, but the world and love aren't perfect. And love is probably the only fall one never gets up from.

Candice never gave me a reason not to trust her; any other man would've gladly put all of their eggs into her basket. I wasn't any other man. I was a young man with trust issues, now facing a life sentence. Not only did I have trust issues with women, but I mostly had trust issues with myself. Every part of me so badly wanted to give all of myself to her but I was scared that I would ultimately hurt her. I was right.

By my third month of incarceration, I had fully adopted the mentality of many before me staring down a lengthy prison sentence. I decided to keep my options open and get as much time as I could with whoever allowed me their time. I'd convince myself that it would be only a matter of time before I was asking people to "hook me up" and subscribing to pen-pal services. One of the options I kept open was Princess.

Princess was someone I had known before my arrest. We came from similar upbringings and I felt she knew more of what was expected for someone doing time. She would help me with all of the extra-curricular activities I had yet to ask Candice of. And just as all of the illicit activities that yielded in cuffs, I'd eventually got caught, compounding the complexities of trust between Candice and myself.

One of the biggest misconceptions about love is that "it conquers all". Love can validate one's purpose in a relationship, but it doesn't keep people together. Often people believe by loving somebody and showing reciprocity, that it'll somehow keep them free from insecurity and temptation and monotony, and all of the things which can compromise a relationship. It doesn't. Due to the process of socialization, simply being human beings, external factors influence us daily, making our interpretation of the world susceptible to change. Our interpretation of the world changes even more so being in prison – a world within itself.

What is a life without companionship? Simply not a life at all. We as people desire to feel valued and appreciated and cared for; it's adjoined to our sense of purpose, confirming that we matter. In prison, it is easy to not feel that at all – as if we don't matter.

Aside from the reality of those around us-guys turning to drugs and violence due to the absence of companionship – we often initiate backup plans, should the letters and visits stop. It's not right, but it is what most of us that are able to do, do. To society, it's immoral; to us it's survival. I once heard my home girl say "The only way to get over a man is to get under a new one". I also once saw a guy a couple of cells down from me in Upstate Correctional get over his girl by hanging himself. I know that was a little dark, but it's the truth. This isn't <u>Orange Is The New Black</u>; if you don't have something to hold on to it's easy to let go. And that thing has a lot to do with trust. This is what T. Maynard of Sullivan Correctional had to say when asked about backup plans.

"Backup plans are set in place for many reasons; lack of trust is the main one. For example, if a couple always has disputes about how money is being spent, then a prenup might be suggested because of the lack of trust or doubt".

S. Leath of Sullivan Correctional had this to say when also asked about backup plans: "I feel having a backup plan is a priority while in prison because the prisoner is at a disadvantage in the relationship. Some may look at it as insecurity, but having your communication limited to visits, calls, letters, emails, etc., you never really know what your loved one is up to. You can only hope the finances are accurate; that they're being faithful; and that your lady is mentally, emotionally, and physically able to withstand the reality of your circumstances and uphold their duty as a wife. And the reason why so many people in prison believe in having a backup plan is because of their reality. From friends to family, at some point, we all experience being out of sight and out of mind. The guys that we are around are daily reminders of what could've been avoided if they had a backup plan. Somebody either left with their heart or money, leaving them miserable."

To both of these men I've had the pleasure of building with, I salute their honesty. Under the circumstances, it's not easy being vulnerable. To even comment on such subject matter can create complexities within their own current relationships. Their truth shouldn't be used as a tool to condemn but to understand.

I've been guilty of having a backup plan even when I've been completely faithful. I'll elaborate. Remember Princess? After severing ties from my deeds being exposed, my behavior was perceived as corrected due to what was shown. For many years after that and being 100% faithful, both emotionally and physically, I struggled to be faithful mentally. Though I now felt secure enough to engage in constructive dialogue with people from my past (with Candice's knowledge of course), call it the narcissist in me, but enough would be shared without blurring the lines to determine my interpretation of getting "backup plan vibes". Similar to falling in love, you just know. And that was all I needed to know that the backup plan had nothing to do with me not trusting my wife, but not trusting myself. Whether it's an insecurity or simply being promiscuous, before we could get to the middle of trust (which is us), we must first be able to trust ourselves.

Again, love is the only fall we never get up from, which makes it scary. To be in love is to be vulnerable, making us susceptible to being hurt. A lot of the time we subconsciously and selfishly choose to protect our hearts at the expense of hurting others, because of the inability to properly address the lack of trust within.

CHAPTER # 4

CHALLENGES: EXPECT THE UNEXPECTED

During my first 2 years on Rikers Island, especially while in the box, all I did was read "hood novels". All of the main characters were perfect: The men were all fit, had money, and porno yangs; the women all had I.G. model bodies, money, and green eyes for some reason. Only the villains fell short of astonishment. Through all of the perfection attributed to these characters, they were all still plagued by their fair share of life. People still cheated, weren't happy, and several other real-life constructs played greatly in the challenges they faced. Though these were works of fiction, they did prove to me a harsh reality: Life is full of challenges.

We place too much expectation on all areas of our life, even more so on our lovers. We want them to be attentive, affectionate, to be champion lovers in the bedroom, providers, nurtures, attractive, smart, funny, confident, ambitious, spontaneous, God-fearing, and everything else our hearts desire. With all of our expectations, very seldomly, if we do at all ask, what do our significant others expect from us?

Speaking from the position of a man in prison, we're often at a loss in thinking about what our significant others might expect from us. Given our location, we expect fidelity to be given, but we all know by now that line "You know where I'm at, I'm not cheating", doesn't hold any weight like it once did. Our liberated lovers see the deceit of others damn near every visit (different women, same prisoner), and hear the most deceitful stories from sleeping with officers and civilian staff (remember Joyce Myers?), even homosexual activity. Nicole from the Bronx knows all too well the challenges of being blindsided by the unexpected of such relationships after finding her locked-up lover in the visiting room with another:

"In most of my relationships, my challenge was largely being able to fully trust a person. Sometimes it's hard putting all of your trust into someone, not knowing if they're going to cheat or connect with someone else; and if so, are they going to be able to communicate that to their partner, as opposed to letting the disconnect play out into disrespect? In this particular relationship, not only did I fear it happening, but I felt it happening. And then once I witnessed it, it kind of tarnished my feelings about this person; if anybody, I thought he would have kept it 100% (honest) with me. Unfortunately, I guess we all have our flaws and are who we are. Never underestimate anybody".

It's something about trust that seems to be the cornerstone of what a healthy relationship consists of. T. Maynard too shared this regarding the challenges relationship face under these circumstances:

"One of the persistent challenges in prison relationships seems to be trust. No matter how these couples met, whether they knew each other before prison or not, we all deal with trust issues. It's no getting around it. Trust issues aren't just about being faithful, but a lot of things. Finances are one of them.

Whether it's commissary, busting a move, stash, etc., the average dude in prison has every dollar accounted for to the last penny. And a lot of times we get fucked over by someone on the outside that we're depending on to help protect our funds. In here, naturally, you will trust your wife to stand on business, but you never really know a person".

Though from just a reasonable perspective, Nicole's and Mr. Maynard's experiences of having "trust issues" derive from compromised expectations. I think the overall consensus would agree that it's normally sound to not want to be cheated on or duped out of money; however, I feel it's more gratifying in the long run to rely less on failed expectations as to understanding. By use of objective thinking we find clarity and understanding of behavior in its entirety; having expectations makes us susceptible to disappointment and letdowns.

Another major challenge that many couples under such circumstances are sure to face is knowing how to effectively communicate. Not only do our love language change when entering prison but also how we communicate.

Often Candice would become angry with me for missing something she said over the phone because I would be too busy surveying my surroundings. This would then lead to us going back and forth: me, explaining to her the dangers of prison; her, explaining to me the need to make the most out of our limited time. We were both right, yet equally wrong in our conveyance.

We couldn't gain any understanding because we couldn't get past our expectations. I expected her to prioritize my safety, while she expected me to (as she should) prioritize her time. Two different people, but ultimately wanted the same thing: Security. This understandable yet less severe challenge compared to the likes of money mishandling and infidelity, would turn fixable communication into irreconcilable differences. The snowball effect. I'm not alone here; Mr. Leath of Sullivan Correctional seemed to have had his own "nothing into something" bouts due to ineffective communication:

"One of the most frequent challenges I've learned with my wife while incarcerated has been the miscommunication between the both of us. Miscommunication on both ends of the relationship equals disaster. And while in prison, given the limited communication, phone calls aren't enough to reach each other; you have to connect face to face. The slightest sign of miscommunication can cause arguments, then turn to name calling, and place even more stress on an already stressful situation (loving with limits.

Dealing with loneliness is also a challenge. My wife's behavior changed over time from not having me around physically. Now she has more responsibility which can be overwhelming for one person, and that causes more challenges, such as spending quality time together. She even has less time for herself, which makes us both feel lonely".

There are challenges in every relationship, no relationship is perfect. However, I believe the biggest challenge presented under these circumstances is time itself. Trust and communication are things that can improve with time; there is nothing that can remedy the challenges of *time* itself.

For time isn't promised nor can ever be made up, no matter how much we wish to, nor by the magnitude of our efforts. I've spent 14 years to date away from my wife and children. All of the riches in the world will never equate or make up for what those 14 years took from us: 14 birthdays and Christmases without me; no teaching my boys how to ride a bike or the oldest to drive; no daddy daughter dances for my girls; no essential support (except marginal financial relief which comes with increased mental and emotional detriments due to all of which comes with, providing the mode of support. More on that later) for my wife; no fundamentally sound example of not only what a productive household looks like, but simply a normal one.

I won't say I haven't been able to constructively reach my children, but the profound intangibles needed to effectively contribute to their development have been greatly limited due to not being able to **reach** my children.

The trauma that comes from the various aspects of just a

visit can present its own set of challenges. You can never prepare yourself or your family for what you all may encounter, which can have a profound hindrance on time spent together. Unjust search procedures, environmental anxiety, exposure to lewd and suggestive acts, and sadly even monotony can be the detriment of what should be a "looked forward to" experience.

Leaving your loved one behind never gets easier; in fact, for some, it even gets harder. I can't forget the officer's unprecedented ability to make this experience either enjoyable or dreadful, yet nonetheless a memorable one. I will never forget the day an officer told me in front of my family that my daughter couldn't sit on my lap, as we bonded almost normally.

I say almost normally because it was an unscripted, organic moment that couldn't be duplicated, yet worthy to be placed in a Hallmark card or a commercial, but was ultimately overshadowed by the realization of "best intention, wrong condition". One of the few and only times I had a moment just as sacred and precious as a child's first steps or talks of the "Birds and the Bees", was taken from me without force or finesse.

I often joked "The only thing a dude ever took from me was advice". But that day, that officer took my moment. It's a moment that no amount of time or money will ever let me recapture. It's also a moment that my family and I realized that none of my achievements nor the fact that I volunteered as an Osborne Association Clerk, helping ensure enjoyable experiences amongst other incarcerated individuals and their families in that very room did not grant me normalcy but a reality check. It was also the moment that I realized that time was omnipotent-equally powerful in bringing us together as it was tearing us apart. I had to be different. I had to assure us all that this was only a moment in time, and that in no time will truly be our moment. I had to reinvent myself.

CHAPTER # 5

The slammer, the big house, the can, college, and even the Army for those of you that have small children. Though there are many names for the Department of Correction, to the lost, it's undoubtedly the school of reinvention. After receiving a punitive decision rendered by judicial officials for the condemnation of societal decree, this is often where one comes. This is where Detroit Red became Malcolm X; where Chris Wilson wrote his Master Plan; and where I rediscovered myself.

No matter one's moral compass – whether driven by positivity or the acquisition of ill-gotten gains-prison seems to breed "being the best" mentally in almost all its occupants. It's like there's no in-between. You either become a beacon of decorum or a better criminal. You're gonna be advanced at something for sure. I only know one person that was the exception.

One of my closest childhood friends, very early had found himself in the middle of this conundrum. I remember being 14 and getting on a free bus with his mother and younger brother to visit him at a juvenile detention center somewhere in upstate New York. When he saw us, he looked the least bit concerned nor bothered. That bothered me. Conscious of still being an at-risk youth, it was as though he'd now internalized and embraced his environment. He was an "all-in" criminal.

I wish I could say my friend turned his life around and went on to do wonderful things but he didn't. He would embark on a life of criminal behavior, perpetuating the statistics of those coming from impoverished communities. His lawless lifestyle, many would assume was best suited for a controlled environment such as prison, but that wasn't who he was.

His troubled childhood plagued by drug addiction, neglect, and limited resources accelerated his unaddressed trauma, cultivating his path in life. He truly became a product of his environment, and only a select few develop the efficacy necessary to make it out. Did my friend have choices? Yes. But you can't judge the choice one makes when you don't know the options they had to choose from.

In prison, you only have 2 choices: You either adopt or become consumed. I've witnessed the most strung-out crackheads become pivotal religious leaders amongst their respective communities while putting on 70 lbs. of muscle in the process. I've witnessed the bullied become bullies, and the "gangsters" become victims. Though most of those who enter these walls do so lost, they won't be for long; prison has a way of quickly defining you before you even have a chance of finding yourself.

I came into prison lost. I didn't know if I wanted to gangbang, find religion, or even live. I would become so enraged every time I'd ask myself "Who am I?" I honestly didn't know. All I was certain of was I didn't deserve my freedom – at least not then.

I believe people to not only be the crux of understanding life but also the validation of life's purpose. I believe people come into our life to show us exactly who we are, lending to our innate ability of moral reasoning. The purpose of one's life can't be measured by individual achievements and accomplishments, but by the profound impact we have on the lives of others. It's all intertwined. My spiritual enlightenment only came once I was able to remove myself from the equation of purpose and ask a different question: Who did I want to have a profound impact on and how? Only then did my spirit shift and my true identity began to take form.

To my children, I wanted to give them pride and drive, and the meaningful love required to transform their weaknesses into their strengths; to my wife, I wanted to be her healer, protector and provider, all while giving her a reason to smile every day; to my mother, I wanted to give her confirmation that she'd done an amazing job as a mother and that her hand in raising me commendably raised many more; to the women that loved me, I wanted them to realize their impact on me, and the pillars of positivity that were built unfortunately from pain, that none of it came in vain but with great purpose. And then when I was finally able to ask myself once more "Who am I?" Now, I was confidently able to respond *a servant of the people* – the lost, the squares, the criminals, and anybody to whom I can constructively bring value to.

Before my newfound sense of purpose, I once told my wife that a man would never ask his lady to bring them "the bag (prison contraband)" if he truly valued her. During this enlightenment process of reinvention, you know what I asked my wife? Yup. Bring the bag. Did it prove I didn't value her? No. though this was a clear contradiction of earlier beliefs, I still wanted to provide and protect. It was a part of me that always existed. And though at this point I was exhibiting signs of true growth and development, I was still a man in progress.

Being a man in progress, I guess the shamefully conscientious side rationalized my morality off of what I asked her to bring. I asked for performance enhancement pills, not the typical heavy request such as weed and dope. And though she was against it at first, I don't think it was solely love that ultimately influenced her decision; it was also her own reinvention of becoming a "prisoner's wife".

When loving under these conditions, it isn't just the

incarcerated conforming and converting, but the liberated as well. Candice undoubtedly knew the relief I provided didn't come from the 14 cents I made hourly, but from good intentions despite how it came. I'm sure that too shifted something in her spirit. It exposed her to the moral imperfections of a prisoner and was also why she ultimately said yes.

I was a man that wanted to live up to the indoctrinated construct of what I believed a man to be, while conscious of being remnants of the man I'd wish to reinvent. I was a complicated man, nonetheless an honest one. The making of who I was becoming, coupled with her interpretation of prison life based on her own experiences were changing us.

Our reinventions at times were difficult to adjust to: it was like getting to know someone all over again that you already knew. So, when we would see certain behaviors that we weren't used to seeing, I believe it made us question each other at times, creating periodic spats that tested us greatly. By learning to respect and understand each others new-found individualities, we were fully able to allow our reinventions to form. She was no longer the dandelion in need of my protection but had blossomed into the strongest woman I'd ever known.

There's no how-to manual for being the ultimate "prison husband" or "rider". There's no way to define who your significant other will become during this ordeal because you can't. All things are susceptible to change; what matters is how you will respond to change. Will you faulter to adversity or overcome it? Will you be able to handle the change within yourself?

CHAPTER # 6

TEMPORARY FOREVERS

If you made it this far, then lucky you. When it comes to locked-up loving, as Meek Mill once rapped "It's levels to this shit". We all love the infancy stage of building a profound connection – visits, poetry and other creative tokens of affection, the attentiveness – but after a while, these building blocks lose their shine. It's not you; it's simply monotony.

See, we (the incarcerated) never get tired of visits or physical touch because it isn't promised. Telling our neighbor to "courtesy flush" at least once a week is more promising than counting on a visit for most of the incarcerated. Here, we have a different sense of appreciation for time and value all of those "institutional luxuries" bestowed upon us. And just as we value these tokens of affection as you all (the liberated) do too, eventually, we'll both want more. You all will eventually grow tired of guessing what we're going to wear, or going home sexually frustrated. The highs and lows of this weekly routine will undoubtedly lead to one – if not both of you saying those 7 words that embody the apex of frustration "I can't take this shit no more". When you're here, providing you're in a state that can assist, temporary forevers will be that next level the two of you will be aspiring for.

One of the things that most married couples of such circumstances strive for is temporary forevers: trailers, fuck trucks, or the politically correct term, conjugal visits. Yes, the idea of being alone, unsupervised, and intimate with your forever person, it's everything. It's one of the greatest ways to normalize, as well as validate the progress of one's relationship under the circumstances. It's also a great incentive to promote positive behavior while motivating one's effort. For the liberated, temporary forevers also give them a glimpse of what life together can look like. Beautiful right? Even with all of the wonders, it doesn't come without its challenges.

The institutional counts performed on these privileges don't just affect the incarcerated but our loved ones as well. It's a systematic procedure used to ensure security measures, yet embed the conceding of control due to its requirements-standing, lights on, fully dressed in state-issued attire, and being asked to give your name and DIN number. I get the purpose of the counts, but why can't I just answer the same phone the officers call to inform me to send my family out in 30 minutes? And why must I be fully dressed in state attire at 6:45 am? Will my pajamas mistake me for a civilian? Most of all, why must I do this four times a day while trying to connect with my family? It kills the moments created and reinforces the unneeded need to promote control. Though one's undeniable positive behavior granted them this privilege, none of it will go without acknowledging the establishment 4 times a day.

Another challenge many face in reaching said apex of incarcerated interconnectedness is the physical aspects of intimacy. Though many probably won't admit this, the lack of physical intimacy between lovers can create barriers such as a distorted view of romance, especially for the incarcerated. One can be inept romantically yet sexually versed enough to satisfy. If you're starving, a Snickers will satisfy you, but the ultimate goal is being fulfilled.

Prison is a melting pot of toxic masculinity. It breeds emotionally confused men, unable to differentiate sex from love, nor understand romance altogether. We're exposed to all of these erotic magazines that influence our desires of how we should please our women – if not just ourselves - so, when we do get the opportunity, we act off our influences instead of listening to the words not spoken: Body language.

We want to do all the nasty shit that people get paid to do. Trailers cost money; she's probably not paying for a foot on her face (Shout out to Rocko Sifredi), while "making love". And if she is, at least let it build up and earn the planting of said foot.

One of my guys who went on his first trailer kept talking about all of the moves he was going to put his wife in, not once speaking of stimulating her mentally. The harsh reality is she doesn't have to go 2 blocks without being offered some dick or having some random person air-dropping her a dick pic in her iPhone. Dick is cool, but dick with substance is better. It's fulfilling. Bring the security of knowing you make her want to keep the lights on, and that that got-damn emasculating count might disrupt the moment but not the experience.

After all that, then it's ok to check some things off your "fuck it list". It's about finding balance, and understanding how being deprived of intimacy while exposed to such vulgarities can impair one's ability to love appropriately. Pleasure and fulfillment are 2 different things. Roses and rabbits might make her climax, but she isn't taking a 6-hour trip for it.

The last thing I would like to touch on when blessed to participate in such privileges is the goodbyes. This can very well strengthen or weaken ones relationship. Saying goodbye on a regular visit can be hard; imagine getting a glimpse of what life can look like, then factor in the realization of how fast time went, and worst of all, how much time your locked away love have left before your forever isn't temporary. That's not something many truly ever adjust to.

14 years in and it only gets harder letting her go. These unsupervised privileges allow me to showcase the reinvented

version of me-dotting father, attentive lover, and ultimately a man worth waiting for. But for now, we both just wait for our next temporary forever.

CHAPTER # 7

WHY I STAYED – BY CANDICE HARRIS

Today is my birthday and the jobs holiday party. I'm not in the mood to attend but I don't go out anymore. Anyway, I decided to attend.

At the party, everyone is mingling and I spot the place where I needed to be as comfortable as possible. I took a seat on the sofa and mingled with co-workers, at least the ones I knew. Then he sat next to me and introduced himself. I thought he was handsome but also thought he was full of himself. We conversed briefly when another co-worker sat abruptly in between us. I thought how rude of her as he got up and left. Well, there goes that, he wasn't coming back. But to my surprise there he was again.

This was my first time seeing him there. I never knew he worked at the hotel and assumed he was a guest of someone until his brother whom I knew in passing let me know who he was. I spent the night speaking to him. It was getting late and I told him I was about to leave. He walked me down and snuck a little kiss in. We said good night and went our separate ways. I was intrigued and wanted to know more.

I couldn't wait to go to work just to see if I would run into him and check the temperature of things. I saw him that morning in the employee cafeteria. We spoke briefly and I gave him my number. For the life of me, I couldn't remember his name.

We spoke that same day on the phone. This was different from any other guy I had ever had an interaction with. He seemed attentive and just so comfortable with himself, it was refreshing. I was content with my current situation of being single but I was intrigued by him - his swag, his mystique just had me drawn in. I felt it was us against them. I saw so much potential in him, in us.

Why I stayed? People ask all the time that very question. Would you leave someone if they had cancer? No. It's the same for me. Honestly, I had no idea what I was getting myself into, how hard this journey would be, the ups and downs, those good days and bad ones, the random females, the lonely days, the depression.

As I stated before, I met my now husband before he became incarcerated. We shared a life before so I had no intention of letting him go. Who to say if he didn't have a backup plan? But those thoughts didn't enter my mind until I was already in too deep.

I didn't know that there were duties expected of a woman dealing with someone in prison. I thought that if you loved someone then you do things for them out of love, not as a requirement. Some men choose their partners in this prison relationship based on what they can get and not on love. It's hard to know the difference when he's so attentive to your every need; when you can check the mail and receive a 2-page letter every day; when he sends you little gifts like a drawing he had made especially for you. Now you are on top of the world and this world only has the two of you in it - or so you thought. Now your world is completely shattered when it hits you that you are not the only woman but you're so stuck. Some will call it survival for them, and others will call them dogs. Do you call it quits and have yet another broken home out there, or do you stay and fight? That's a decision only you can make. Is love enough to see you through, and do you have what it takes to make this relationship a real one?

My life became this (prison), planning for the next visits, trailers, keeping the kids connected to their father as you want for them what you didn't have. You become a prisoner yourself as your life now revolves around his and his needs and your dreams for a family. You see, when a man does what they call a bid the woman does one as well at the same time.

Taking these long bus rides to see him and even longer ones back home became my life. But this is what I wanted and this is what it entailed. You lose friends and some family members, as they don't understand the dynamics of it all. All you have are the ladies – the faithful riders of those vans as they too are in the same struggle as you.

Now this is not a bed of roses by a long shot. There is always someone gearing up for the position of prison wife. I don't get it. Like it's a badge of honor or something. I'm not a "prison wife" but a wife to my husband. This is not something I can do for someone I met through a pen pal service. It's way too much that goes into this for this sort of relationship I think to last.

Granted, men and women cheat, but not for me. It feels worst when the one you claim to love is building an entirely new thing with another from the inside. There are no dates, just an emotional connection. Maybe it's for the bag (prison contraband), a package, some money, or the infamous backup plan. I believe every man in there has had one when they got in there. They claim they don't know if you can do this time or have what it takes, but what it means is you will not be at the beck and call with visits, packages, phone calls and letters. Your life is now being revolved around their needs and controlled by them. Congratulations! You are a new parent with bills and more bills.

Imagine your man, the love of your life, kissing, feeling another woman, and doing some of the things you do together on a visit. All for the bag he says. She probably wouldn't be here still.

Coming from two different walks of life this was not the

norm for me. I wanted a family, and that was stolen from me when one early morning my front door was met with a loud banging. That would be the last time I saw him in our home. My world ripped from me. And now as I chose to go on this journey with him, he conduct himself like any other man out there, selfish. Still, I stayed because I loved him. Did he mind fuck me or was I in love with the idea of having a family and proving the nay-sayers wrong?

We as women sell ourselves short by not requiring the things we need from our men and settling for anything. You should be honest and open, so boundaries are set. Think about it, if you get into a situation where you are doing the same thing, he will not go for it. So why do we? Love and hope are crippling but it's what we hold on to.

CHAPTER # 8

*THE PRICE OF LOVE: IT
GET GREATER LATER*

As hard as it was to read my wife's sentiments then (2020) it's just as hard today. I wish I could tell her that, that was then and that I'm a different man today; I wish I could replace her insecurities (many of which I've contributed to) with grand gestures of appreciation and the fulfilled promises I envision daily; I wish she could see herself through my eyes and understand that I see her and truly value her worth; that REAL EYES REALIZE REAL LIES, and that the truth of our love is one that most will never understand, few will ever experience, and that we could never doubt. It's uniquely ours.

We often hear that cliché "honesty is the best policy", yet faced with it, rarely do we readily wish to accept all of what it entails, especially when that honesty is coming from our significant others. Though honesty can lead to unintentional conflict, the sentiments that one truth derives should be processed thoroughly in hopes of gaining clarity and understanding. One's truth shouldn't be used to weaponize nor vilify.

Individuality allows us to appreciate the aesthetics of being different; however, amongst our significant others, relationships under these circumstances allow us to endure many of the same challenges just in our own way, and with different options and moral guides as to how we navigate them.

The "bag" which can be as little as $100 worth of weed can be the detriment of a 15-year relationship. Though the risk doesn't amount to the reward, this is indeed an abnormal environment where abnormal rules apply. No matter how much time couples have together under these circumstances, the "bid" that you two are undoubtedly doing together will be done in two different prisons, with two different sets of rules, ultimately resulting in two different experiences.

It's easier to point out the holes in the truths of others compared to admitting the flawed truths of ourselves. For me, it was hard to recognize the objective of coming home, without engaging in behaviors that could've led to the extension of my sentence; or how the deprivation of physical touch coupled with the overexposure to pornographic material contributed to over-sexualized desires, rendering me inept romantically; or how my wife's very present presence (visits, trailers, letters, etc.) at times inadvertently showed me just how much I was forgotten by others, revealing hidden insecurities that influenced a lot of the poor decisions I've made, ultimately breaking Candice's trust and greatly compromising our marriage. Even then the love couldn't be doubted; still, I can't tell you why she stayed.

For our "riders", I'm sure it's hard not to psychoanalyze every aspect of us to ensure that we're not engaging in stigmatized behavior: down low lifestyles, women on the side, manipulative agendas, and anything counterproductive to coming home a reformed man; or the ability to express sexual frustration – if not act on it – though giving your hearts fully (Please don't misconstrue hearts and parts). And in some cases, especially those who have repeatedly found themselves in a cycle of failed relationships, it's hard to own the unhealthy feeling of satisfaction from being in a relationship that grants a level of control, most women will never experience with a liberated lover. It's often on men's terms (it's gonna hurt to admit), just as most relationships in general. Despite the circumstances, which is usually by the helm of men, it's all due to society's acceptance of hegemonic masculinity.

I am not a "prison husband", but simply a husband to my wife. I've witnessed this bid transform my saint, my dandelion, into constructs more callous than the most notorious of prisoners. She has watched my emotions take on the conductivity of all things conniving, to unwavering compassion and a great sense of generosity, based off of what the day entails. Our marriage was commenced amongst convicts and strangers and a justice of the peace that stood us up previously (more on this in the next book) and our understandably confused-looking small children. My best man was a dude from Harlem who sported face tats. Our cake was an individually wrapped Hershey Cream Pie, straight from the vending machine. Though this wasn't the perfect setting, we weren't perfect people. Nobody is.

Though we were married in prison and most of our complications came from being in prison, our love wasn't defined by prison. I believe by conceding to the label of "prison husband" or "prison wife", you subconsciously suppress the profoundness of your impact and allow your relationship to take a backseat, prioritizing prison over each other. By putting each other first- never defining ourselves as prison spouses and accepting our reinventions- it allowed us to weather the complex challenges of our prisons. It allowed us to not just hold on to hope, but believe that it'll get greater later.

Life and time are the only two things we can never repay. With that being said, be mindful of those we choose to spend ours on. Ask yourself if the people we're loving, love is backed by viable resources – reciprocated through behavior, reciprocated without incentives, reciprocated honestly, reciprocated through efforts, and reciprocated through pain. Again, reciprocated through pain. I'll explain.

As mentioned before, one can never truly experience Love if

not for pain. We have to be honest with ourselves, that by loving someone, they can hurt us. We also must acknowledge in times of loving someone, the admission of our vulnerability can allow us to hurt others, especially given the insecurities and complexities of confined connections such as these circumstances.

Your mindset must view every day as presenting either a new journey or a new challenge: From both, we gain experience, but depending on how we look at it will determine how we interpret the magnitude and efforts of how we approach each.

When you allow the **purchase** of both your life and time to someone you deem **worthy**; by embracing and accepting their pain (truth in its entirety) is the only way the **withdrawal** of such a profound **investment** can ever **repay** the love each other will spend lifetime trying to find. It **costs** and comes at a **price**, that no temptation, imperfection, incarceration, or any form of hate could ever **liquidate**.

16 years together, 14 years of incarceration, 11 years of marriage, and a lifetime to go. It only gets greater later.

ACKNOWLEDGEMENT

There are too many to appropriately be named in the process of writing this book. Though this book attempts to shine a light on the challenges of a particular group of people through my journey, this book was written before I ever stepped foot in a prison. It started as early as my first steps.

To my mother, with whom I undoubtedly first experienced love, I thank you for not only giving me life but the lessons to go along with it. After the death of my father, there were a lot of things that I felt robbed of learning. And though you couldn't teach me how to be a man, you gave me more than enough as well as the freedom needed to find purpose. For what is a man without purpose? Not a man at all.

Candice, without you I don't know where I would be. Your love consumed my broken spirit and morphed into a phoenix, only to rise from the ashes. You saved me. And though I could never repay you it won't stop me from trying.

My children: Jadon, Reyhan, Montana and Cayden. Each of you have provided me the much-needed sources to never conceded to defeat. Jadon provided me the creativity to step outside my comfort zone; Reyhan challenged my discipline to choose life over vice; Montana's tenacious resiliency showed me that defeat (the feet) was made for taking a stand, and Cayden's brilliance and own testament showed me that we are not who they say we are.

My father, though your life was cut short due to a brain aneurysm, greatly limiting our bond, I'll forever cherish the moments shared. He taught me that a man's instability should never get in the way of his responsibility.

Early on, being unable to identify my unrealistic expectations of measuring up my love interest to my mother, I'd sabotaged several good relationships. Though I've gained a lot from those losses, my personal growth and development wouldn't have been possible without these experiences. To you all, I would like to both apologize and thank you.

During my incarceration and continued pursuit of higher education, I was fortunate enough to have met Professor Weber of Suny Sullivan. I will never forget how you challenged me to dig deep and truly use *writing as a way of healing*. You helped me cultivate the confidence of finding my voice.

I would like to thank all parties involved for their participation and contribution with the illustration of loving under such conditions and the challenges faced.

And lastly, though many start with acknowledging you – I bear witness that through God all things are possible. Through her (yes God is a she) grace I am here today. The reason I chose to close out with her is because I didn't start this journey with her in my heart, but today I do.

ABOUT THE AUTHOR

Joshua Harris

Joshua Harris is a Suny Sullivan Graduate and also the Founder of GR8 (Getting Results In Eight Weeks) workshop where he promotes positive lifestyle choices.
He's a father of 4 and at the time of press, currently incarcerated.

RELATIONSHP RATING EXERCISE

Anything worth having is worth fighting for. And when it comes to matters of the heart, its not uncommon to find you and your significant other doing more fighting with one another as opposed to fighting for one another. The many different layers of love – from vulnerability and building security, to discovering each others love languages – can be very challenging. You may even feel as though everyday you have to fight just to prove your love. That's fighting with doubt. You fight everyday to protect your love. That's fighting with purpose.

I can't tell you how many times Candice and I was fighting with doubt yet going the distance. My incarceration played greatly in the longevity of our union, but was it also the only thing keeping us together? And if it wasn't, how were we to validate our love, ensuring that we're fighting with purpose?

One day, while my wife lied asleep on one of our "Temporary Forevers', I became overwhelmed by a number of different emotions. As I watched her sleep peacefully, I was both happy and hurting. We were in a really good place; I just didn't know how long we would be in it.

Understanding that everyday wasn't going to be sunny, it seemed as though as of late, our differences struck a different cord – a more permanent one. It was almost as if we both didn't have anymore fight left in us. But I wasn't ready to throw in the towel – and neither was she. Then out of nowhere something came to me: something that would later become the relationship rating system.

How the system works is quite simple. Each of you, preferably in the beginning of the week will share not only your requirements of one another, but also your triggers; at the end of the week you will then give your partner a score from 1-5 (5 being the best) as to how well your significant other met your needs for that week. By focusing on being what your partner needs from you on a weekly basis, with receiving a good grade as an incentive, it'll subconsciously condition you two to make those desired changes more permanent. You can't expect to have different results when doing the same thing. Try it and see if this exercise works for you or not.

Thank you for your time. And behalf of Candice and I, we wish you all the best as you continue to love through barriers and without limits.

9 798892 176354